Sidelights, Fanlights and Transoms
Stained Glass Pattern Book

180 Designs for Workable Projects

by Ed Sibbett, Jr.

Dover Publications, Inc.

New York

Sidelights, Fanlights and Transoms Stained Glass Pattern Book is a new work,
first published by Dover Publications, Inc., in 1987.

DOVER *Pictorial Archive* SERIES

Manufactured in the United States of America
Dover Publications, Inc., 31 East 2nd Street, Mineola, N.Y. 11501

Library of Congress Cataloging-in-Publication Data

Sibbett, Ed.
    Sidelights, fanlights and transoms stained glass pattern book.

    1. Glass craft—Patterns. 2. Glass painting and staining—Patterns. I. Title.
TT298.S43   1987   748.5′022′2   86-29179
ISBN 0-486-25328-7 (pbk.)

Publisher's Note

For well over nine centuries stained glass windows have adorned spectacular churches, important government buildings and stately homes of the affluent. It was not until relatively recently—during the Victorian era—however, that stained glass increasingly was used as an integral part of the design of middle-class, single-family residences. Traditionally, a favorite location for the placement of stained glass windows was on and around doors. Today the domestic use of stained glass windows as ornamental sidelights, fanlights and transoms continues to be extremely popular. It is for this purpose that the fascinating stained glass patterns in this volume have been specially designed.

The 180 patterns, of complexity varied enough to satisfy both the relatively inexperienced and the master craftsperson, represent many styles and themes: Art Nouveau, Art Deco, florals, birds, geometrics and more. Each offers creative challenges in color design, glass cutting and construction. The patterns can be used singly or in conjunction with each other to dress up any door, or they can be adapted for many other stained glass applications. Depending on the size of the intended project, the patterns can be reproduced in larger or smaller sizes as necessary.

This collection of patterns is intended as a supplement to stained glass instruction books (such as *Stained Glass Craft* by J. A. F. Divine and G. Blachford, Dover Publications, Inc., 0-486-22812-6). All materials needed, including general instructions and tools for beginners, can usually be purchased from local craft and hobby stores listed in your Yellow Pages.

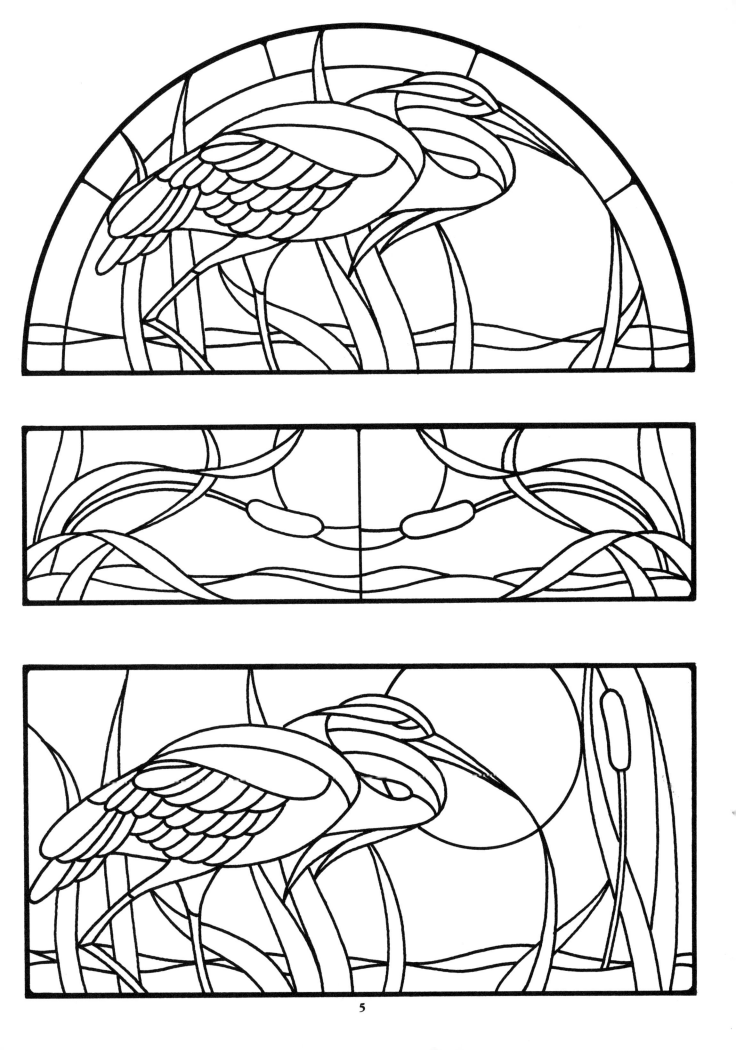

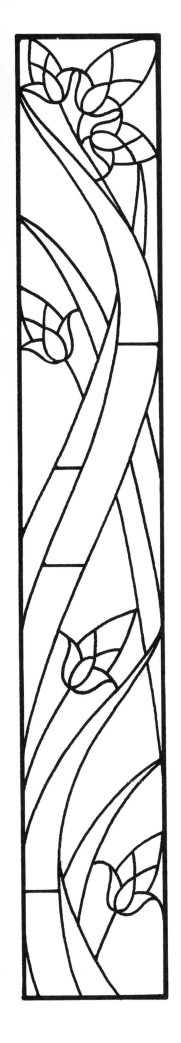

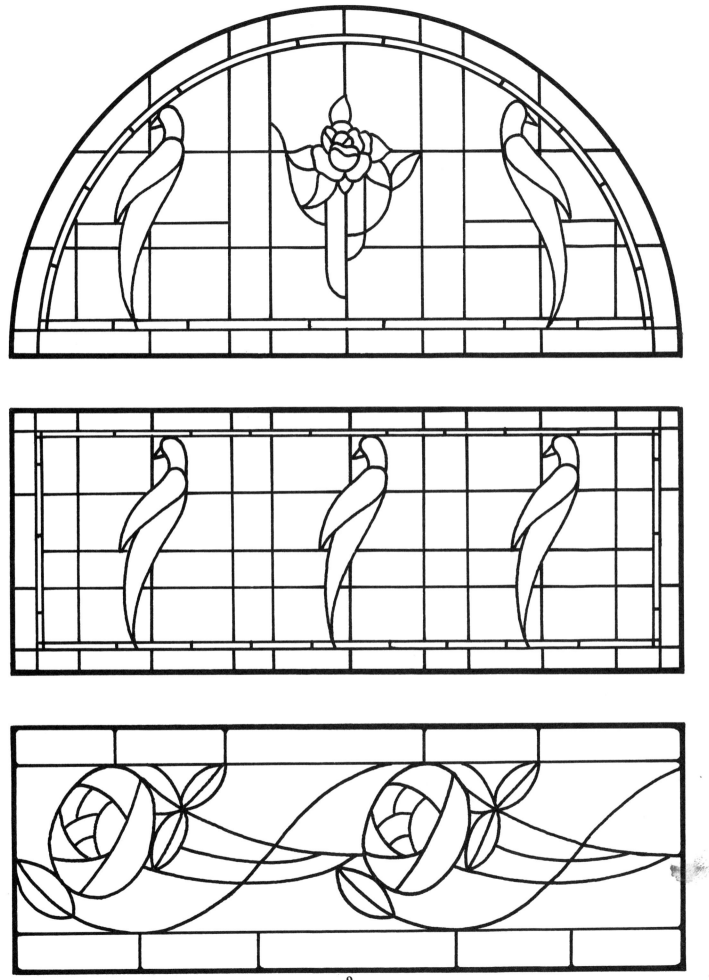

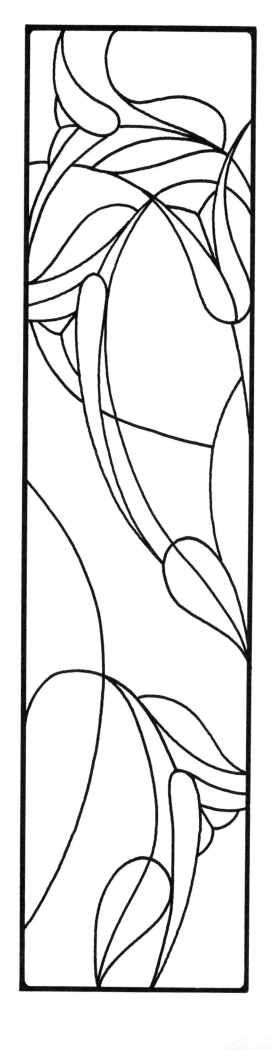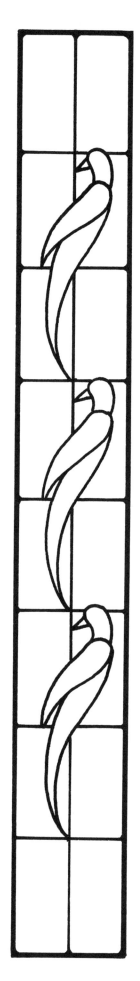

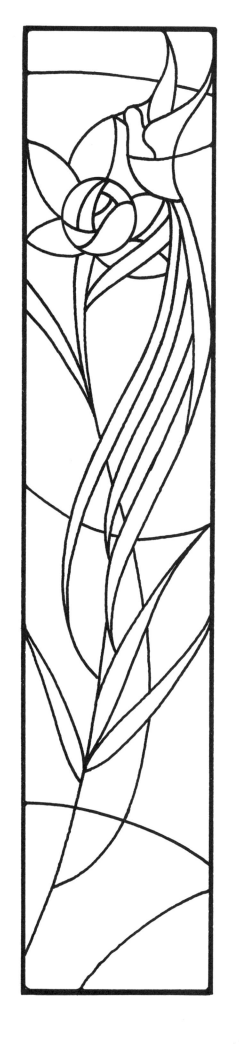
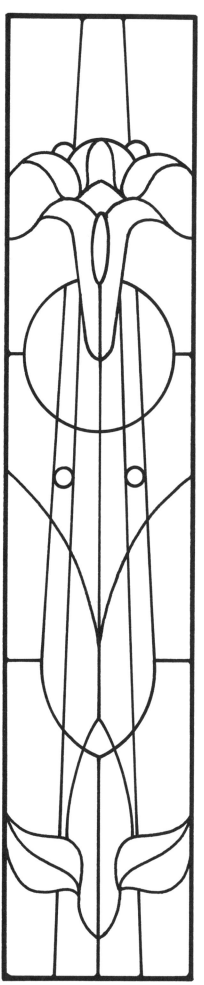

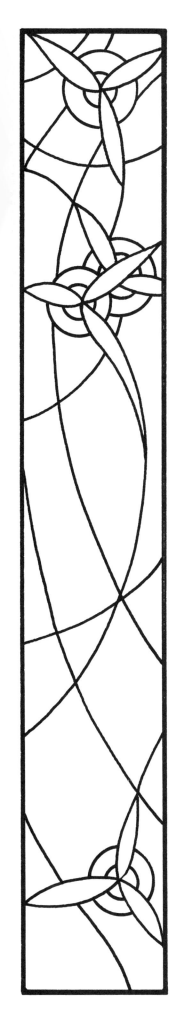

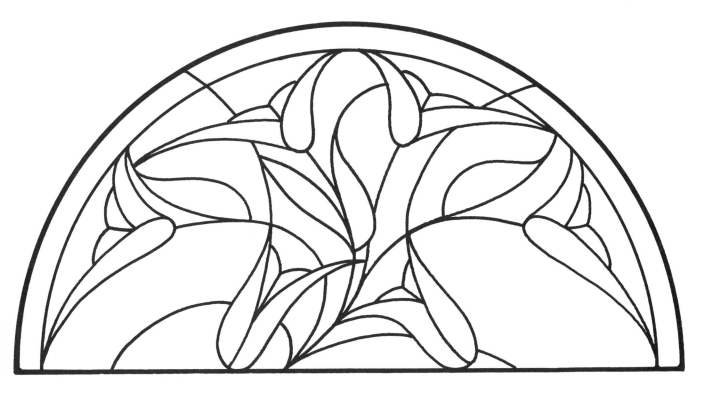

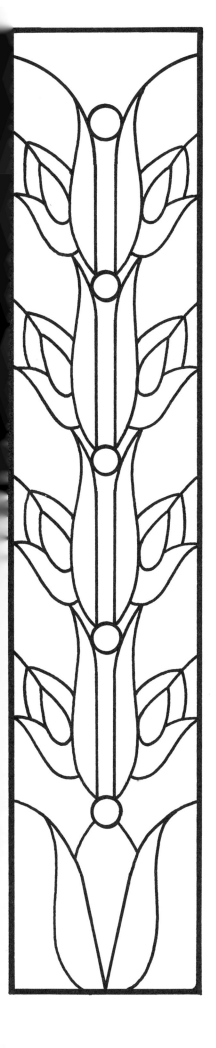  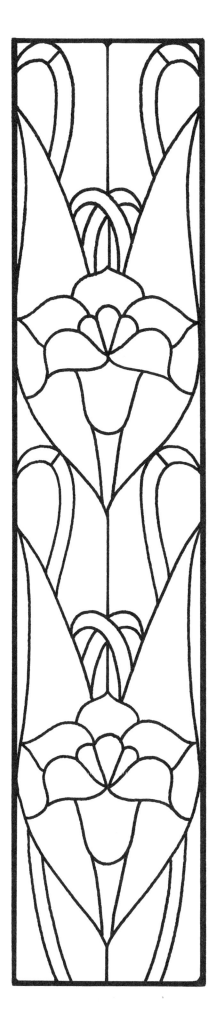

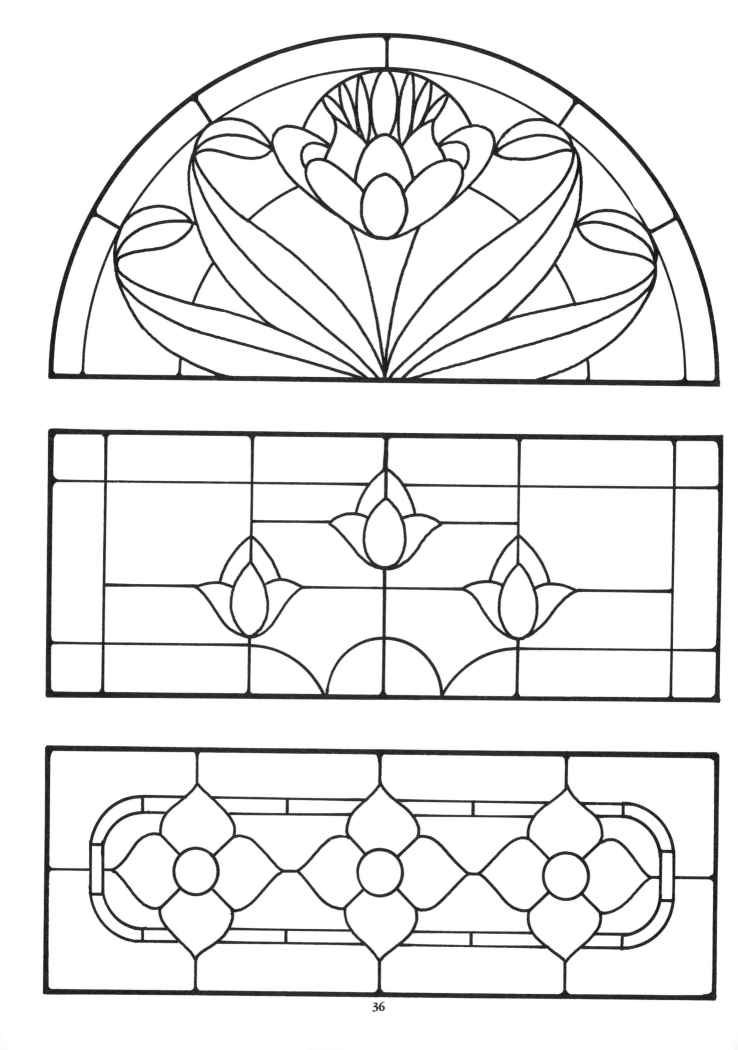

43

51

53

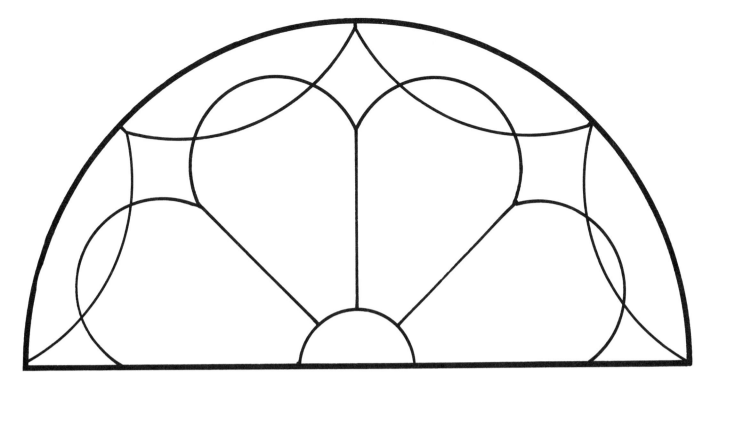

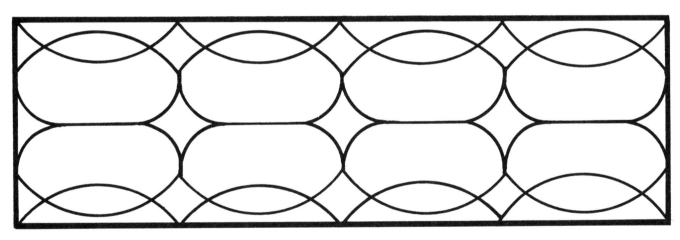

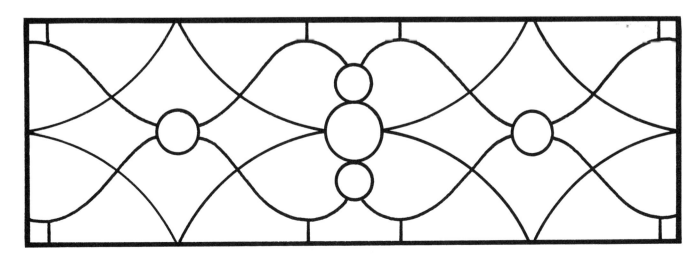

57

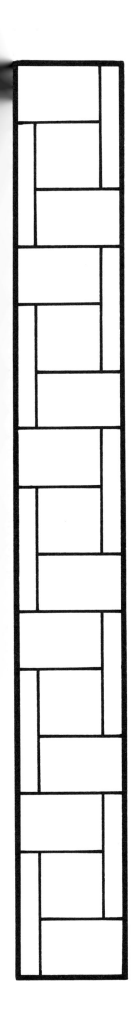

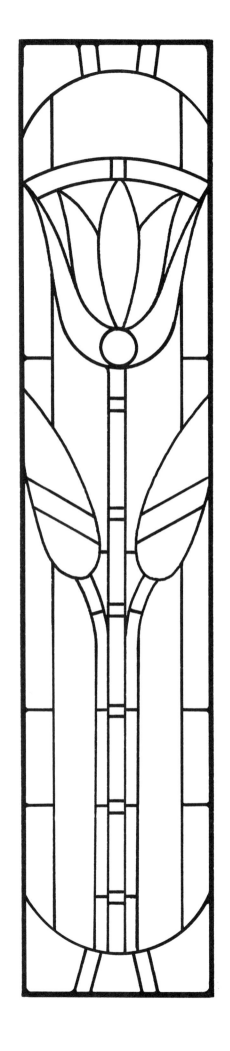
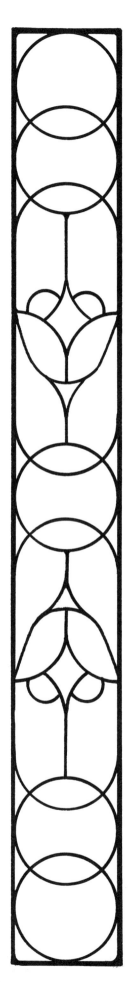